AF335328

113
114
115
116
117
118
119
120
121
122
123
124
125
126
127
128
129
130
131
Ballantine's
12

AFTERIMAGE

BY

DAMON KRUKOWSKI

✳

WITH PHOTOGRAPHS BY
NAOMI YANG

UGLY DUCKLING PRESSE :: DOSSIER
2011

Portions of this text were first published in *Amplified*, ed. Julie Schaper and Steven Horwitz
(Brooklyn: Melville House); *Poses: Cédrick Eymenier*, ed. Matthias Alaguillaume
(Paris: Éditions Ordet); *The BSC Manual*, ed. Bhob Rainey (New Orleans: NO Books); and
Figuring Color, ed. Jeremy Sigler and Jenelle Porter (Ostfildern, Germany: Hatje Cantz).
Grateful acknowledgment is made to those editors, and to Anna Moschovakis,
editor of the Dossier Series for UDP.

Library of Congress Cataloging-in-Publication Data

Krukowski, Damon.
Afterimage / by Damon Krukowski. – 1st ed.
  p. cm.
ISBN 978-1-933254-88-3 (pbk. : alk. paper)
I. Title.
PS3561.R826A38 2011
811'.54 – dc23

                          2011034979

Distributed to the trade by Small Press Distribution
www.spdbooks.org

First Edition, First Printing 2011
Printed in the USA
Ugly Duckling Presse
The Old American Can Factory
232 Third Street #E-002, Brooklyn NY 11215
www.uglyducklingpresse.org

CONTENTS

I.

BOOKS, MY UNLUCKY OBSESSION

II.

DEAR FRIEND

III.

VISIT TO THE LA JETÉE BAR

IV.

DEAR POET

V.

FLYING DOWN TO RIO

AFTERIMAGE

{1}

How quickly the tales we tell ourselves and each other, the small rationalizations, the hopes and excuses, even the snatches of songs and poems, build in our lives not to a crescendo, but into a wall that blocks the view. We sit as in a garden, the walls protect and define the space, but whether we turn to one another or inward to peer at ourselves, these calcified stories impinge our movements, our heads and hips no longer swivel freely. And then one day some bit of story breaks loose, swirls through the body like a fish finally past a dam, lodges in a small crevice of the heart or mind, and brings the novel to an end.

These were my thoughts a few days following a conversation in which it seemed nothing that wanted to be expressed, could be. Or rather nothing that was expressed, was received as such. All sides were left wanting.

The landscape slipped by the train. I felt like that bit of story, hurtling toward and then into the most intimate parts of the city. That evening, in the dark, my friends played music to a room of strangers. They sang,

> *I am riding, I am riding*
> *Forthcoming from the inside*

And I was struck by their reversal of the image I had earlier conceived: my friends' feelings, from the inside, were exploding outward toward the crowd. Using the story's own force, they have parried its thrust, and put its power to use. The story is a dynamo.

The next morning, I finally give my parents a copy of my book of poems. These poems are the destructive bits of story in my life, swept together like crumbs. In the first one, my father builds a wall, but underground:

> *Eventually we covered the trench over, and said*
> *a prayer*

I cannot watch their reaction. I give them the book and immediately leave.

In Seoul, Korea, the rain has stopped, we are walking with our hosts after dinner. The small square in the center of this neighborhood is filled with young people cooking on Bunsen burners, playing badminton, drinking beer. The makkoli seller arrives, pushing a gigantic cart stacked with white bottles. "Sake?" I say to B. "Or milk?" he suggests. The makkoli seller spots B., six feet tall, stops his cart and strides up to him. The makkoli seller is equally tall. He addresses B. in a few words of broken Japanese — "Delicious! Healthy!" — and then something in Korean that makes the women in our group laugh. The men are pushing us away. "Taste it! Korean rice wine," he explains, this time in English. B. shakes his head no. The makkoli seller pours the white liquid into a paper cup, eyes locked with ours. Still smiling, he pours it on the ground.

The temptation to write a little each day — the invitation, the promise, the imperative — has often presented itself. Just a little, and by the end of a year imagine how much writing you will have done. But why write so much? Why add to the endless march of days, recorded or not? Why not one page per year; or better yet, one per lifetime. But why that too.

Why any page at all. Why add. What wisdom it would be, not to write.

✳

Lisbon, some months prior to Korea: walking in the dawn because the bed was too uncomfortable for sleep. Bakeries unlocking their gates. Streets wet, whether from rain or from having been washed I do not know. Wandering, but taking care not to get lost — tracing the route seen from above, as on a map. I stumble on Pessoa's favorite café, pointed out the day before. A coffee at the bar: *"O melhor café é o d'A Brasileira."*

I realize I have not been wandering. This back and forth across the map — does it not trace a familiar route? There is no war; on the contrary, our travels for music depend on peace, predictability — Spain and Portugal were only added to the itinerary once the Fascists were truly gone. But the refugee's path is likewise an opportunistic zigzag. Looking for asylum. Longing for a coffee at the bar.

The city awakening. Morning sounds of no fear.

✳

Chronology is another temptation, another trap. Why write each day; why write in order of the days. These are bourgeois ideals of efficiency, productivity.

✳

The medicine show arrives, and we unpack its carefully collapsed props from a set of nesting crates. All is arranged for transport foremost, maximum effect second. A red top hat packs flat as the plates in the moveable kitchen. A headdress of ostrich feathers is revealed, on closer inspection, to be painted silk and tin. Every material dissembles; even many of the foodstuffs are ersatz, whether for economy, longevity, stage use, or all three. These jars of beans might be stones. A loaf of bread, one slice removed, is in fact paper and paste. This ham is made of wood; but the bacon, equally hard, smells sweetly of smoke. Ambiguity protects the goods from pilfering — who can be sure which hammer bends like rubber, which chair collapses at the slightest pressure, which pot is filled with grease paint and which with cooking fat?

✳

Another city with its face smeared in burnt cork. Its noises might be anywhere near the sea: Barcelona, San Francisco, Taipei. A resident would recognize the idle of domestic cars, the type of warning whistle one can ignore. But the visitor falls for them all, without question, without guile. The visitor is an audience.

Once the visitor starts a routine, the city becomes the audience. This is why the performer carries a city with him, packed in crates.

How to cut through the routine of received ideas, habits of thought — cut through like a train through the city. Look to the backs of houses, disused lots, community gardens, concrete riverbeds. Don't look to faces — faces are smeared in burnt cork.

We rehearsed in the garden. It was midday, too hot to be outside. Behind us, two men work to erect a backdrop painted with characters — "wind" and "sound" — but the frame

they have built is unsteady, it keeps falling over. We feel the
heat on our instruments.

Go ahead and mention the book you are writing, like Ovid's
writings in exile — he describes the situation of the book,
and writes the book, without any disjuncture. Both are the
truth. The truth of the situation, and the artificiality of it.
The wandering, and the route it traces.

*

I should mention the book I have already written, as well: a
book of poems. These poems are the destructive bits of story
in my life, swept together like crumbs. In the first one, my
father builds a wall, but underground:

> *Eventually we covered the trench over, and said*
> *a prayer*

A few months after this was published, my aunt E. — my
father's only sibling — died. The day of the funeral, after we
had watched her casket lowered into the ground, my father
said to me: "It reminded me of your poem, about the time

13

I hid in the root cellar." I was confused. Which poem? "The one about the time I hid in the ground and didn't come out for three days — you know the story." (I did not.) "When L. left." (His nanny, sent away when the war started.) "The smell of the earth — it always makes me think of it."

That day he also said: "There's no one left, no one who was there."

Clue to the power of silent movies: Clara Bow's career was ruined when sound revealed her heavy Brooklyn accent. This accent undoubtedly helped her silent performances, however.

We crossed Spain, and crossed it again. Cities rose up out of the plain, and fell back again into nothing. We crossed Spain, littered with the memory of cities.

We drive into the center of one, Valladolid. Everyone in the city has forgotten everything — this is because the Fascists had been there, and no one wants to remember them.

How do you sing to an audience with no memory? That night, we try to sing songs like those cities on the plain — rising up out of nowhere, and disappearing just as quickly. Why add to these people's memories, if they want none.

Singing like this feels like singing into a heavy black void.

The sax player upends a bottle of water into his horn. A watery solo follows: bubbles of air emerge from the mouthpiece, and float up to the ceiling.

I realize I have described this experience, some years before. It was a poem written in the second person, perhaps because I had not yet myself lived it — a memory written in advance of experience. Does that make it a song for Valladolid? I will retitle it now:

Valladolid

Experience of singing is for you an auditory one, you have never sung aloud. You cannot remember doing so, at least. Singing while asleep is possible, even beautiful, the pitch is perfect and breathing effortless. Nevertheless no sound emerges during such performances. The breath you exhale is suspended, little bubbles escape as from a swimmer but there is no room for air, the space inside is completely full with nothing, and motionless. When you wake, breathing is normal but awkward. Your throat is scratchy as if from yelling. Glycerin is useful in lubricating your unused vocal chords. You have been under water a long time.

{2}

Dear Friend,

I am wandering through another city on tour, this time it's Paris, in the neighborhoods where it feels like bits of the world have gathered, swept together like crumbs: from the Maghreb, from West Africa, from the Subcontinent. Smells of roasting coffee float out a doorway, the sign tells me from Brazil. Aren't these Rimbaud's ideals, come to life and (how ironic for the adventurer) come to Paris? The triumphal arch at the top of the Faubourg St.-Denis, lit by the orange glow of an unseen sunset, is to the mechanized city a barrier. But on foot — in human scale — it is a monument to all the people and all the things that crowd around its base.

And my own feelings: why not let them crowd around? What is it that I am keeping at the perimeter, outside the barrier?

In a dream, Titus's arch in Rome is (still) buried up to the inscriptions describing the destruction of the Temple. I touch the reliefs. The ground below is not solid; it is a glass walkway, constructed for tourists. Loudspeakers announce approaching troops. And then I am in bed at my grandparents' house, having that familiar dream again — a dream so much a part of my experience, it can even be a dream within a dream — it's the one where the screen door, which leads out of the room and directly into a field, will be my escape. Bears and crickets fill the field beyond the door. There is another loudspeaker outside. Animated like a face, it grimaces and shouts directions.

Gare de l'Est. Gare du Nord. Church of the West. Southern Seas.

When I saw the garden at Ryoanji, I thought: it makes the flow of a stream into an image. Similarly, the flow of ideas is a literary trope ("stream of consciousness"). But the flow of the street — the barber dusting off a chair in preparation for a client — this doesn't feel to me like an image or a trope, it feels like life itself. Is it because this is the only kind of life visible to a person on the run? You have to sit still to contemplate the motion of a stream. Perhaps also to observe one's thoughts. And sitting still is a privilege of peace.

The Surrealists made use of this flow of the street in their art, it's true — I'm thinking not of their automatic work, but their works of imitation: *Immaculate Conception, Hebdomeros, Adventures of Telemachus*... In these the metonymy of the street — the signs, slang, snippets of conversation — stand in for the more discursive antecedents of history, literature, philosophy. Just as the coffee beans I smelled today are Brazil.

Is it that I feel each refugee is a nation? Each carries all we are to know — here, in the flow — of that other place. And each has borders — barriers. That's the cold war that follows every hot explosion. Scatter people, and they grow icy hard, as lava turns to stone. Bumping along the road, and against one another in the street, those stones are ground to pebbles. Crumbs.

An actress from David Mamet's company once described to me a technique they call, "as if." Do not play the Queen of England, play yourself *as* the Queen of England. No artifice = the greatest artifice. We know you are not the Queen, but if you are being true to the moment then we know what you are thinking and feeling as the Queen; all that is left for the actor is to accomplish what needs to be done in the scene.

Isn't this game equivalent to the literary idea of imitation? When Breton and Éluard simulate madness, the effect of their work depends on our knowing that they are not, in fact, mad. In the same way, Buster Keaton does not satirize, or ironize, the melodramatic hero. He simulates the hero — he casts himself in the role *despite his unfitness for it.*

Rimbaud did the same, out there in Aden. He could have bought coffee in Paris.

I realize now why I am writing to you: I feel unfit to tell this story. But I have been cast in the role regardless.

This letter, with all its literary debates and anxieties, struck me as strange, even artificial. It is artificial: the artifice of "as if." Do not play Kafka, play yourself *as* Kafka. No artifice = the greatest artifice. We know you are not Kafka, but if you are being truthful then we know what you are thinking and feeling; all that is left for the writer is to accomplish what needs to be done in this book.

What Is To Be Done? The title is so compelling, I've kept it on the shelf all these years, just to read the spine.

Others? *The Wretched of the Earth. The Origin of Family, Private Property and the State. Mules and Men. The Interpretation of Cultures. Language as Symbolic Action. The Language and Thought of the Child. Growth and Structure of the English Language. The Forest of Symbols. Writing Degree Zero. On Collective Memory. Zakhor.*

Their import seems so obvious now — my bookshelf is like one of those embarrassingly overdetermined dreams in Thomas Hardy. How could I not have seen it?

N. wants to write herself a letter from Paris, and tell herself how it feels to be away from home, away from her family.

Certainly it is easier to write if I can believe (pretend?) it's private. This must have been my motivation for a pseudonym, before I first published. R. talked me out of it. Careful not

to divide things too much, she warned — there might not
be enough to go around. But she probably didn't imagine
I wanted to keep the work secret from family; there was
nothing in those first poems (or was there?) to indicate that.

And could I have kept it secret? Had I published under a
pseudonym, and later divulged it, I would have found myself
in an even worse situation: no secrets from family, all secrets
from the public. And what I craved was the opposite: all
secrets from family, none from the public. I will have to live
with no secrets from anyone.

Kafka's letter to his father, written but never sent. My letter
to N.'s father — trashed so that I would not be tempted to
send it. My letter to my father… You are reading it.

The morning after arriving home from Europe, the phone
rings and N. picks up. "Are you deeply depressed?" says my
father, without announcing who it is. "No, are you?" she says,
and hands me the phone.

My self-recriminations come flooding back: chief among them that writing like this is not literature. This is not a book. Is it a letter?

Cf. Ovid:

> *...though the words are the same, I write to different people —*
> *one cry for help, but many addressees.*
>
> (*EP* III.9)

And my ambition, at its most grandiose: not to write a book. To write a non-book.

Cf. Robert Smithson, site and non-site. Eva Hesse: "non, nothing, everything."

The room we rented in Paris, already slipping into nostalgia. The saffron curtain. The Christmas lights hung on the mirror. The mantelpiece with a drying bouquet. The small utensils we bought to cook our meals.

By a rice field at night, our friends pull the car over so we can listen to the frogs. We are near the mountain where we will spend the night. The room at the inn is so fragile, it feels like it was made in a children's art class — paper, sticks, and glue. The light flickers from the insects flying around it, casting shadows. Steam rises from the building next door. We bathe, then sit together in a more brightly lit room, drinking sake and telling ghost stories. Next morning, a walk down a mountain path — there are plants we have never seen, growing on each side.

✳

Before returning home, N. and I each write ourselves a letter, posting them from the airport along with our *détaxe*.

> *I'm gonna sit right down and write myself*
> *a letter*
> *And make believe it came from you*

It is early spring. At the far end of Walden Pond, N. and I are by the railroad tracks, listening to a loud buzzing sound. We cross the tracks and walk down a path that leads to a clearing. There is a small marshy pond sitting in a bright bowl, the area is loud with peeping frogs. The sound blots out everything but the light.

{3}

At the Museum of the Moving Image, an exhibit on nineteenth-century motion-picture games explains this principle: when vision is interrupted, the mind retains an afterimage of what the eye had seen. If a light illuminating successive images flashes, the darkness between causes us to merge this afterimage with the next, which we sum to one in flux rather than two in succession. If a light is constantly shown on successive images, we see only a blur. That is: *interruption is necessary to the illusion of continuity.*

In the car driving home, I think this must also be the structure of memory — images that we retain in isolation, but sum together as they flash in our minds. Perhaps this is also the structure of dreams. Dream logic emerges as we work to make sense of the succession of images, separated by blackness.

Thus Chris Marker's *La Jetée:* memory presented as discrete images (stills). If we cannot recall the image immediately before or after, we cannot recall motion. Nevertheless we work to sum these images together, and make sense of them in time. The logic of memory is the logic of trauma.

✳

Visit to the La Jetée bar: C. has given us directions out of a dream — "Take the only street with trees." The area is not far from our Shinjuku hotel, but in a direction we never walk. (I remember friends saying on our first visit, "Don't go that way.") We keep to the main streets, to avoid getting lost, but see no sign of the old drinking district he had described. And then: a street with trees. We take it away from the neon, into the darkness. There are blue tents in the bushes, shelters constructed by the homeless. It is a weeknight, the street is otherwise empty. We come to a crossroads — in one direction, more blackness — in another, the old ramshackle district of bars. C.'s directions worked.

Wandering among the bars, La Jetée is still hidden. We ask another "mama-san." She graciously leads us there. It is up a flight of stairs. No way to look inside before opening the door...

At the Tenement Museum on the Lower East Side — interior rooms, banned from use by building codes, were walled up rather than changed. Some later reopened, with interior windows added to satisfy requirements for light and air...

When I sang about this, I imagined someone still living inside when those interior rooms were re-opened. I associated the darkness of these spaces with a lost language.

> *Hide my eyes from the light*
> *And say the words that I can't understand*

Adapted to the singer's point of view for a later chorus, this becomes:

> *Hide the light from me*
> *And say the prayers that I should understand*

Sitting with my mother at the kitchen table, I ask about the jacket I saw in *It Happened One Night* — both Clark Gable and the sleazy character on the bus wear the same cut, they are only tailored differently. She knows the name of the jacket: Norfolk. How did her father buy his clothes? Were they on a rack? Thinking about it, she recalls the view from their apartment on Riverside Drive, windows facing upriver — warships at anchor. They moved to 86th Street when? It must have been very soon after the war began, because she remembers being on 72nd Street when she heard about Pearl Harbor, and what would she be doing on 72nd Street when they lived on 86th Street? The wind off the river was so strong she had to walk home backwards from the subway on Broadway. Suddenly she remembers: a tailor used to come to the house, and fit her father for clothes. "A Jewish tailor," she says. "Where did he find one of those?" I say, and make her laugh.

Show at the New York Public Library of 1960s mimeo books and magazines — this thought: that a "poetics" should enable one to identify poetry in new places, not just in other poems.

This is the test of a useful poetics, because arguing about poetry itself is circular and pointless — we already know all those things are poems, from someone's point of view. No need to establish the hierarchy from our perspective.

So poetics does have a function — it is poems that do not.

Wasn't this Cage's insight into music?

✳

On Beacon Hill to see an early music performance of Sephardic songs — the venue is a building I'd never noticed before, an abandoned synagogue on the north side of the hill.

The musicians are in the center, on the bima. There are two galleries for the audience, at right angles to one another — these must have once separated men and women. The space has the haphazard dimensions of the interior of a city block, but covered over with a skylight. There are several layers of painted decorations on the crumbling walls. Palm trees.

During the performance, the singer chooses to face one gallery, and then the other, in turn.

✳

At a restaurant, Dad says to me, "Since we see you so rarely, you should order the caviar." I suggest we split it — I think

maybe he wants the caviar, which is why he's urging it on me?
— and that way it will cost no more than two other dishes
at the table. No, no, he says, he doesn't like caviar the way
I like caviar. Anyway, it always makes him uncomfortable.
Uncomfortable? Yes it reminds him of the trans-Siberian
railroad. "You know the story," he says, as he always does
when introducing a story he has kept to himself. It seems
that on the trans-Siberian railroad, if a train was coming
from the other direction, the one he and his family were
on would be diverted to a sidetrack, where it would wait
for hours, even days. While there the conductors would lock
all the doors and windows — because wherever they were,
however remote, people would eventually arrive, with plates
and cups, begging for food.

Once, my father and his family were in the dining car as
the train sat like this. They were served caviar. Caviar?
Apparently the meals came with the tickets. "It wasn't
luxurious, by any means, although after prison camp it was
certainly a shock." And while they had the caviar before
them, people were banging on the window glass, hungry.

I say I'll have something else. He insists. So I insist we split it.
We do. He has the tiniest taste. (I eat the rest.)

Saw Sunny Murray with Sabir Mateen, at the Unitarian Church in Amherst: Sunny Murray played as light and free as his records — that skittery, constant, calming sound. But seeing his body language, I felt he was simultaneously playing traditional tunes in his head: ballads with breaks, turnarounds, solos. When he started a song on the brushes, alone, I was sure he was waiting for Ben Webster or Lester Young to join in. And he hummed — atonal humming, like the memory of a beautiful song without the melody or the changes. Just the space for its feeling.

As I leave my parents' house, my father looks away. Is he hurt? Depressed? There is so much he wants from me, I think. Or so much he thinks he wants from me. The guilt I take away is like cases in my hands.

*

Takuboku Ishikawa's *Romaji Diary* — like Campana's *Orphic Songs* — Boethius's *Consolation* — the dream of a writing so complete that prose and poetry are equally needed. Also Pascal's *Pensées* — these are thoughts, events, that must be recorded, and the form they take is a mirror of that necessity.

And if I wrote in a language no one could read, like Takuboku, could I include it all? Takuboku gave his diaries to a friend and his wife, and therefore to an audience. So from whom was the *romaji* shielding him? His family — his rivals — but not from those closest. Circles widening out.

Dream: with Dad in some kind of basement cafeteria, I am questioning him about something and his face clouds over. He says there are family secrets I don't know. Like what? I am pressing. Like his middle name, he says. Face becoming completely closed and dark, shrinking away from me behind glasses. "The middle name is Magarshack. Like the writer," he says. Like the translator, I ask? "The *writer*," he says. The distinction is lost on me. Out in the street, 86th Street walking west with Mom, I say Dad told me his real middle name. "Don't do that!" she yells at Dad, who is suddenly there too. Why not? I say. "Now you know he is born *under a blue sign*

34

star," she says. It is a frightening idea. Then in a highway restaurant with Dad, in Vermont — it is divided over two stories (!), with multiple dining rooms, antiseptic. He tells me how he once worked there — it was a fine restaurant then — while commuting to Lincoln, Nebraska. This is somehow connected to the secret of the middle name. He shows me how far it is on a map. Then, he says, he stopped (commuting? working? *writing?*).

John Wieners walks into the Poetry Room at Lamont Library to give a reading. He opens a book (his own) and begins. But then he stops, and looks at the page like he has never seen it before.

I recognize something in that gesture: looking at one's work, and finding it at times intimately familiar and at other times foreign and strange.

If Wieners's work weren't true, it would never be familiar to him. And if it were always familiar, it wouldn't be so true.

My own reading at Lamont Library. N. is there. K., who has been staying with us, is also there. A few students.

I spent so many hours in this room, years ago, listening to recordings of poets reading. Stein. Stevens. Ashbery.

The sunlight is low, and the room is overheated, as always.

I am overcome with feeling. Something other than pride. It is hard to read clearly, because for a moment I am near tears. There is a recording being made.

Do we only tell each other's stories? Ask others to tell our own? Can we tell our own? Or is that what stories are for — to tell someone else's, and allow another to tell yours?

I find bits of stories everywhere in Boston:

D.L. MOODY
CHRISTIAN EVANGELIST,
FRIEND OF MAN,
FOUNDER OF THE NORTHFIELD SCHOOLS,
WAS CONVERTED TO GOD
IN A SHOE STORE ON
THIS SITE
APRIL 21, 1855

Harry Houdini
(Erich Weiss)
1874-1926
In memoriam to the great Artist
and past National President who performed
one of his well known escapes from this bridge
On May 1, 1908.
Society of American Magicians
Boston Assembly Number 9

THIS ESCALATOR IS
DEDICATED TO THE MEMORY OF
COUNCILOR HYMAN PILL
FRIEND OF THE SUBWAY RIDER
AND ALL MANKIND

And the plaques of memory, those I saw in Paris as a child —
to the martyrs of the resistance, fallen on this spot — nearly
always with flowers fresh or recently faded. The bullet holes
in the walls fascinated me then.

✳

In Paris now, I take note of a different set of markers:

> 165 enfants Juifs de cette école
> déportés en Allemagne durant
> la seconde guerre mondiale
> furent exterminés
> dans les camps nazis.
> N'oubliez pas.

This in the Marais, at the beautiful stone school building
behind the Marché des Blancs Manteaux. Inscribed over one
of the two entrances, it says:

ECOLE PRIMAIRE
COMMU. DE J' GARÇONS
ISRAELITES
MODE MUTUEL
FOND MUNICIP. JUIN MDCCCXLIV

Over the other door, the stones are effaced:

ASILE ECOLE PRIM.

ALE DE JEUN

SRAELITES

I look up *asile* — "refuge" (cognate: asylum). Or is it a fragment?

✳

Who memorializes the survivors? They have to die before they can be remembered. And when they die, the ones who remember them — but not the events they survived — will write their stories. If they ever told them to anyone.

A plaque is for the dead; an effaced inscription is for the living. Or: the living are an effaced inscription.

✳

In Boston, it's as if we live in a utopian novel about the future — its vocabulary rooted (and limited) by the past's projection. The 1930s steel towers of Post Office Square, the

39

Italianate parapets of State Street, the granite office "blocs" named for once prominent families… each an old idea of what should be here, now.

The present and the future may be as entangled here as in Japanese. I sang this once about Walden Pond:

> *We went walking in circles today*
> *At the edge of water, of now and never*
> *We're never in time*

But it could have been equally about Logan airport: flat earth with low hills beyond — the setting sun exactly as in the luminists' paintings — the use of the land exactly as Henry Adams might have predicted.

Long walk through neighborhoods not meant for walking — overpass to train tracks, CSX loading facility, car repair shops. And the domestic life hard by: sagging wooden balconies on the backs of brick buildings, "Boston International Gourmet" with signs otherwise in Russian, "Allston Tropical Market" with a few Brazilian products on largely empty shelves — imported soap, Easter candy, magazines, an enema kit, plantains, meat, packaged bread.

A girl makes silly faces at her mother through the curtains of a ground floor window. I think of something my mother told me only recently — how in New York during the war, my father's parents' friends would bring to the house all their bills, official forms, and documents, for my father to translate, fill out, make calls about or otherwise fix. He was still a boy, but the only one who had learned enough English. He resented it, she said. Was it the responsibility he disliked? The tie to the emigrés? The constant reminder of their troubles? Or perhaps: the use of his skills for their ends.

A wag has placed a plaque to Quentin Compson's suicide, on the bridge back to Cambridge:

Quentin Compson
Drowned in the odour
of honeysuckle
1891-1910

Lyric: only a moment amid a life of failure. Life of success would be epic.

*

N. and I play my mother a Sinatra record, with orchestrations by Gordon Jenkins. I had predicted she wouldn't like it. She doesn't (she prefers Nelson Riddle). "So 'Hearts and Flowers'!" she says. It reminds her of Radio City Music Hall on a Sunday, when she was a child. Why? It was so dreary — everyone dressed up in a horrible way (though she remembers her own royal-blue winter coat with pleasure) — and the place was too big, too many people. And can you believe it? Her brother mentioned just the other week how much he had loved it there, how he would go every weekend. How could he? Maybe if you had to see a movie the day it opened…

But didn't she like the movies they played?

Yes, of course — but better to see them at the Alden, Loew's 83rd, or the Beacon — which was big, but not like Radio City. She and her best friend would go together and refuse to sit in the children's section, instead asking someone on line to accompany them through the door. "Otherwise you were surrounded by horrible children, and watched over by a matron." There they would watch the film more than once

42

— just stay and let the feature begin again. "You tried to come in for the start, but sometimes you missed it, so then you waited for it to come around. And then you'd get sucked in all over again…"

My father adds that he remembers being in the balcony at Loew's 83rd, alone at the noon show, watching *Sergeant York* with Gary Cooper, Walter Brennan, Joan Leslie. And then staying all day, watching over and over. He says he learned English that way —

I look up *Sergeant York*. It was released July 2, 1941. How many weeks or even days had he been in the country? I have to ask him what time of year they arrived in New York.

What are these different sections? Each an attempt to tell the story. Each a way to say it all. Each a form that tells a part of the story; or, the same story in a partial way — 1. declarative/narrative, 2. direct address (letter), 3. interior (internal monologue and dream), 4. address to self (diary), 5. lyric.

Cf. Ring construction (Mary Douglas, *Thinking in Circles*)
— AB C B'A' — with (sometimes) an additional "latch"
at the end. Note her ideas about endings: in a ring, the
beginning (and the progress to the center) determines the
end — it is a foregone conclusion, you know from the first
half the signposts that mark your progress to it. She makes
comparisons to pattern poetry; and to Leviticus, formed in
the shape of the Temple.

That is, look to the beginning — and the center — to
determine the end.

For front?

> *Books, my unlucky obsession, why do I stay with
> you...*
> > *Isn't one well-earned punishment enough?*

> > > Ovid (*Tristia* II)

✳

Back in Paris, in very bourgeois surroundings this time —
piano practicing upstairs — startled madame in the entryway

when I opened the door — children arriving at school in the morning, led by the hand — flag over the entryway.

My own bourgeois background reflected as in an antique mirror; the European upbringing my father carried with him.

Finding it so hard to write, to continue this work without questioning it in the most fundamental manner. Isn't it just complaint? Decadent, self-indulgent complaint?

Beggar outside the bakery this morning, as I buy croissants. I give him the change. This is only further implication: I am now the right age, wearing the right coat, and carrying the right croissants, to be giving a beggar small change. And writing? Every man in this neighborhood is eating croissants, and writing.

Writing through — as therapy? This too smacks of complaint. And yet, writing as consolation — Boethius — this seems like something else again. The consolation of poetry: poetry may not enter this text, but it might address me, in my situation. What does poetry have to offer? What Cage points to: acceptance of the sounds I find. I happen to find this endlessly yammering voice of criticism. Listen to it, as to the piano practicing upstairs, the children's voices in the street, the garbage trucks in the morning. It is still yammering, but in combination with these other sounds, does it become something more?

I hear a chorus of silent reproach — more like prayers in a church, than thoughts in a library. It rises with the stillness here in the afternoon, after lunch and before the children leave school. It is in the ashy sky with its dribbling rain, which brings it back down to the balconies and roofs, draining it into the gutters and washing the streets.

N. says: write more. Don't just edit.

I am in a hurry to finish, however. Why? To rid myself of this task. (To whose end, this use of my skills?)

Show in Paris at a lovely underground bookstore, "On the Margin" of the bourgeois city, in a North African neighborhood slowly filling with hipsters. The audience is sweetly curious, and attentive. A boy from Colombia tells me afterwards: usually everyone here is too cool, or aggressive like Dada. You brought an honesty we needed, he says. My head spins a bit. Our playing tonight was amateurish, I thought — we are out of practice, and the sound system in the store was primitive. But honesty and amateurism — these are not mutually exclusive. The boy is so direct, I cannot imagine he needs any instruction in feeling. Is he offering it to me?

Two mystical dreams:

At Pyramides metro stop in Paris, a man builds pyramids of snow, which hover above the ground.

In a plane flying over a mountain, so close to the ground the pilot follows the roads on it, and points out sites such as a man walking below, etc.

C. takes us to Agnès Varda's installation for "les Justes" at the Panthéon.

Varda has filmed two versions of the same set of anecdotes, or fragments, illustrating situations in which people hid Jewish children during the war. One version is black-and-white, filmed to look like a "war movie." The other is color, in dramatically contemporary, hand-held video. The focus here is on the details of normal life: hands, feet, earth, trees.

Everywhere in Paris this time, I find black plaques to the deported children. Each school we pass seems to have a new one — with fresh flowers.

"Les Justes"... such an odd formulation. Nuns and priests figure heavily among them, it seems.

Why only those who helped the children?

Afterwards, C. suggests a café, but then complains that it is "full of disgusting Frenchmen, eating." We go to the apartment where we are staying instead; I make him coffee and we share a galette des Rois (it is the season). N. finds the prize in the first slice, and wears the crown. Seeing her, C. says he regrets not bringing his camera — "This is the second opportunity I have missed this month," explaining that the other was a fight that broke out in the streets between demonstrating firemen and the police.

N. shows him her digital camera and he uses that, taking her portrait with the crown from the galette. The encounter is uncannily like N. with her father.

C. refuses the pastry, explaining that he never eats in the middle of the day. The apartment is across the street from a camping store, and C. remarks that he used to buy his food there — a mix that provides all necessary vitamins and nutrients for the day, in one draught. "Don't you eat raw meat, as well?" N. asks. "Just a little, at night," he says. He truly is a cat.

N.'s insight while in Paris: when she paints (or I write), the mind wanders — if you are afraid of where it might wander, you don't paint (or write).

Amazing view on the flight home — breaking through the clouds over France, the sky blue above a solid field of gray. Glimpses of the North Atlantic — whitecaps — and eventually, the North American coast, entering by the St. Lawrence and tracing its path. On approach to Boston, the Charles is frozen, a light snow makes the shape of it and all the rivers and ponds especially clear. The city huddled against its harbor. Trees everywhere, instead of fields. Highways instead of roads.

Our house this morning, flooded with light. The New England sky. Bare branches all around. We live in a village, truly, not a city at all. Still an outpost.

The retrospection of Breton at Percé Rock, Quebec, 1944. The war is across the sea. A year of forgotten (unknown?) struggles. And his own prose at this moment: placid, nostalgic, even spiritual — strangely (for him) uncombative. Because the real battle was elsewhere?

The world is always at war, its beginnings and endings are illusions. World War II began the moment the first one ended. World War III began as soon as the second one was finished. Haven't we lost count by now?

The world is always at war, because the memory of war is in the present. Has any generation truly known peace? Peace, without an afterimage of war?

Do we even know what peace is, except as the negation of war? Do we have a positive idea of peace?

Would that be enlightenment?

My reluctance to even print this manuscript out... The privacy of the screen is greater than the notebook — it's the feeling that this could all evaporate, like a memory, with an electric shock. What would the traces be? The effaced inscription — the erased description —

My father's feelings — that would be his book. I can tell a story only of his actions. And my feelings.

In New York again — Dad takes us to an expensive meal. The details are repeating. (Is this permission to finish, at last?) Home the next day, N. and I draw the shades in the afternoon, luxuriate in our privacy and peace. Two days later: I slide into a depression, like I'm on a slope of black sand. (Will this force me to stop, regardless?)

The ideal opening: "I hate traveling and explorers. Yet here I am proposing to tell the story of my expeditions." (Lévi-Strauss, *Tristes Tropiques*)

{4}

Dear Poet,

Your non-book arrived. Not by post, exactly. The situation reminded me of something else you once sent:

> *...the letters they wrote were transported by hand, out in the open, from place to place.*

I do not mind your sharing these thoughts with others, even if it's only to reach me. But are you sharing everything that you promised? Did you "include it all," as you say? What are you leaving out, beyond the perimeter? Have you left those things out on my account?

Did you imagine that I require that of you?

Consider the pleasure of picking up the guitar and simply playing — that's what Gertrude Stein felt, writing. I know because she told me. Yes, in a non-book, delivered not unlike yours.

Why not just write about the things you love? Take them — 78s, old movies — and do whatever seems possible with them, or in their spirit.

Halbwachs speaks of memory as distinct from the individual — arguing that our memories are determined by others' recollection, as well as our own. Memory is a social fact, not only a psychological one. Dreams he identifies as memory without society; hence nonsensical, scrambled, non-linear. Social memory, on the other hand, tells a story. It has a purpose; individual memory does not.

Using Halbwachs's terms, is not fiction a form of social memory? In other words: *why are you bothering to tell the truth?*

How perverse that you have turned yourself into an editor. Leaving out has never been your problem.

Rereading Bruno Schulz lately, I was struck by the different tone in his two books. The first (*Cinnamon Shops*), so effortlessly strange and lyrical. It is addressed to no one and stands tall as an autonomous object. The second (*Sanatorium under the Sign of the Hourglass*) is self-consciously addressed to the reader. It is lyrical, too — but as in Agnon, or Chekhov, here the lyrical is presented in order to move the reader, rather than for the disinterested pleasure of its own existence.

Consider the title story of that second book: a perfect dream logic, until the last two paragraphs. (You see, *he* needed an editor).

Music gives you that disinterested kind of pleasure, I know. A gamelan performance, with dancers, in midwinter at Sanders Theater in Cambridge — doesn't it convey both the idea of a symphony, and that of a voyage? The playing in unison, the balance of the instruments, their careful positioning in the room... And at intermission, one of the dancers in full make-up, wearing a camelhair coat over her costume, selling scarves and jewelry at a table.

What did you feel then? Why are you leaving that out?

Schulz, again: "It is part of my existence to be the parasite of metaphors, so easily am I carried away by the first simile that comes along. Having been carried away, I have to find my difficult way back, and slowly return to my senses."

From his truly perfect story, "Loneliness." Study it.

I watched Herzog's *Kaspar Hauser* last week. It too has many lessons for you: in particular, the scenes where he struggles to reason, or to express himself; the puzzle of the tower and the room inside it; the comedy of his debate with church and university; his tears, falling from open eyes.

You sang about that once —

> *And who am I to ask why I've been found*
> *I'm just water fallen down to the ground*

Or was that about me, too?

✳

This letter tore through me, as if I were its envelope.

✳

Is this the consolation of poetry? To make something out of what cannot be used. To say something of what cannot be said.

The effaced inscription resembles lyric.

Is this why I stopped writing poems, stopped breaking lines?
It seemed like it was saying less, rather than more. I wanted
to include it all, so I wrote prose.

But if the subject cannot be spoken of — cannot be the
subject — is not mine to speak about — is not permitted to
be spoken of —

Then the leaving out — the blank spaces — (fill in the gaps)

Saying it all is for the dead. Biographies. Variorum editions.
Plaques and memorials.

And for the living: an effaced inscription. Lyric.

∗

The only remaining question, then: who is living?

{5}

These were my thoughts as I wrote the following poem. It makes use of the language and setting from an early Fred Astaire/Ginger Rogers film, *Flying Down to Rio*. The title reminded me of a story my father once told me, a story he told me fully because it was not his own:

"V., M.'s husband, refused to leave Germany before the war, even though M. herself refused to stay once the Fascists came to power. So M. was already in Paris when V. was arrested. He was sent to one of the concentration camps, it was not yet an extermination camp, this was when they were ostensibly for political prisoners. And at the camp, V. went into a depression, a clinical depression; he could not get up. The Red Cross still visited the camps in those days, and can you imagine, they got him out because of his depression. M. lobbied the Red Cross from Paris, and they got him out of the camp, and out of Germany.

"V. then joined M., first in Paris and then in New York, but his depression remained. Years later, after the war had ended, he went to Brazil to visit E., a cousin who had emigrated there in the 1920s. What he told my father — your grandfather — was that on his way to Brazil, as the plane broke through the clouds, his depression lifted. And it never returned."

When N. and I flew to Brazil on tour, this story became my own. I was not depressed like V., but as the plane broke through the clouds, I felt something change in myself. It was dusk — all flights to Brazil from the US leave in the evening and land in the dawn. The sky had been dark near the ground in Miami, but up above was the orange glow of an unseen sunset. We were flying to São Paulo, that upside-down mirror to New York. The war was over, truly over, and in that moment I believe I felt it for the first time. (However briefly. Because I have never been depressed like V., perhaps I will never recover like V., either.)

I ordered champagne from the stewardess. If there had been caviar, I would have ordered it, too.

Later I would sing about the experience,

> *Flying upside down the earth is blue*

That same song quotes Celan, to represent V.'s depression: *black milk of daybreak.* Because I imagine V. saw dawn for the first time since the camps, as he landed in Rio.

In the poem, the Astaire/Rogers film provides data from the 1930s, because movies are the best evidence I have that there was a world before the war. The last line is delivered by a drunken Astaire, as he watches a parachuter drop from a plane. It is a witness of exile, turned into a punchline. The "gal" of his gag might be any number of allegorical figures — or it might be Dolores del Río, rejecting yet another suitor attracted to "the Latin type."

A LATCH TO THE RING

"I like music, old and new
But music makes me do the things I never should do"

At the Hotel Hibiscus, survivors gather
There were as many paths here as people
Florida? Is that where we are? Oranges, sun?
It looks like Wilno to me.

Songs move faster than planes, level the landscape. Old tunes,
Familiar gestures, same odd use of verbs:
"Eat an aspirin"
Or adjectives:
"Heliotrope coveralls"
Mark the era. It is the thirties. War not yet.

Where are we flying today? Over a mountain,
So low the pilot points out the occasional passerby, uses roadsigns
At the Pyramides metro stop, when it snows
There is a man who builds pyramids of ice
They hover over the ground like a low-flying plane

Crazy nothing — that guy writes songs

"Music makes me," thinks Honey Hale
Yes madame? Pencil.
"Music makes me do the things I never should do"

Shall I lay out your heliotrope coveralls?
We are flying down to Rio for the gala opening of the Hotel Atlantico

All the survivors will be there
They gather wherever we go
We play dance tunes like it's the 1930s
But they do not dance, they just listen
And remember the conflicts that were

Try the Culbertson system, or Lenz
A fox trot, or a polka
Let's show them a thing or three

In Brazil we don't elope; it's bad taste
"You're right — here we belong to our families,
    and our promises —
Even though all we want in the world is beautiful,
    crazy happiness!"

Love is old, love is new
In Rio by the sea-o
The big number is beginning
It's the tune we play the survivors
As they disappear
That is, die off
So accustomed to the deaths of others
And to resisting their own

They need a distraction — use your Brazil nut,
It's song and dance they crave
Like everyone did
When jobs were the problem and food was expensive

My Rio — everything will be okay

Rio by the sea-o

"Gosh, that gal don't care who she gets thrown out of what"